Nina Lemon

Hidden

A Play about Self Worth, Mental Health and Self-Harm

Salamander Street

PLAYS

First published in 2020 by Salamander Street Ltd.
(info@salamanderstreet.com)

Hidden © Nina Lemon, 2020

ISBN: 9781913630584

Printed and bound in Great Britain

10 9 8 7 6 5 4 3 2 1

This play was developed working directly with young people as part of my role as Artistic Director of youth arts charity Peer Productions. I would like to acknowledge the charity's executive and trustee team, particularly Claire Knight and Ed Simpson, for bringing this work to such a large audience as well as Dr. Pooky Knightsmith for her guidance on adolescent self-harm. I am indebted to all the young people who shared their stories with me with such honesty. I would also like to thank the original cast Lucy Barton, Alice Cockayne, Kitty Cockram, Hattie Chapman, Aedan Day, Rosie Horler, Aaron Langford, Mark Notley, Megan Strachan, Holly Taylor-Zuntz and Ethan Todd for their commitment and integrity developing the play and the many other young casts who have since taken this play out on tour.

Handle with Care – A note from the playwright.

My work, as a playwright for Peer Productions, is made in direct response to the needs of the young people whose lives the charity seeks to transform through theatre. I cannot remember a time when young people, youth workers and teachers were not asking me to tackle the challenging topic of self-harm. Uncharacteristically, I avoided the topic for many years, terrified that making this play could, inadvertently, trigger self-harming behaviour. I, like many others, remained silent on the topic while, in both community and youth theatre workshops, I was seeing more and more young people physically scarred by self-harm and began to hear more and more stories of young people being stigmatised by their peers who could not understand why they were self-harming. In 2015, when I wrote this play, the topic was receiving some media coverage with alarming statistics showing that one in five fifteen year olds said they had self-harmed in the previous year and numbers of young people attending A&E for self-harm was at an alarming high. It had become clear to me that our cultural silence was ignoring a problem on an epidemic scale and that, with or without adult guidance, young people needed so very desperately to talk about this often hidden and taboo topic. This led me to contact a range of mental health professionals and to collaborate with adolescent self-harm expert Dr. Pooky Knightsmith who provided script consultancy for this project. I also interviewed young adults who had self-harmed when they were younger but were at least two years into their recoveries, to gain more insight.

It is not possible to make an effective piece of theatre without any risk. This play has toured to thousands of secondary school students in year 8+ annually since 2015 with very many schools rebooking each year. Many schools report an increase in the number of young people seeking help as a result of seeing the play. Teachers tell us that it provides a useful starting point for often challenging conversations with young people and young people tell us that they are better able to both understand and support their peers after experiencing the play.

I approached writing this play with great care and I would encourage anyone reading or staging this play to approach with similar care. Below is a list of things in the play that might be triggering for some young people. This doesn't mean that those young people, who could be vulnerable, should be excluded from experiencing the play, but that care should be taken to warn them and to support them. It is also important to note things that we do not see in the play and that should be avoided in any productions. We do not see anyone actually cutting or burning themselves. Whilst the devastating impact of suicide is spoken about by Chloe's mum and we see Tash take an overdose, suicide should not be presented sensationally or, in any way, as any sort of solution. When I wrote this play, I was worried that it could become very dark and traumatic. I have made efforts to ensure that there is lightness and humour. If you are staging this play, lean into the lighter moments as they are the key to humanising the characters. I also want to remind you that, ultimately, Matt, Sophia and Tash offer three stories of hope and recovery. We know from the very first scene and are reminded each time we return to the festival that with support, like many young people, they have been able to stop self-harming. The message is that recovery is not just possible but desirable.

Trigger Warnings

When we talk about triggers we mean things that could trigger negative feelings or damaging behaviours. Obviously, as everyone's experience is unique, anything could potentially be a trigger.

Having said this there are certain key triggers that we have actively sought to avoid in the play.

In this play you will not see or hear:

- Graphic or explicit details regarding the mechanisms of self-harm.

- Graphic or explicit details regarding suicide.

- Any suggestion that suicide has any positive outcomes.

- Graphic or explicit accounts of sexual abuse or any other trauma.

However, in this play you will see or hear:

- Non-explicit references to self-harm – cutting, burning, hair pulling, laxative abuse and overdosing on unspecified medication.

- Non-explicit references to suicide and the emotional impact on the family.

- Non-explicit references to memories of childhood sexual abuse.

- Scenes containing bullying including Islamophobic bullying and emotional bullying centred on a character's weight.

- Characters who have scars as a result of cutting and burning.

This play is designed with flexible casting in mind to suit casts from 8 actors to 25.

Although, in theory, a smaller cast is possible *(with narrators doubling in each other's stories)* comfortable minimum cast requirements are 9 with 6 female performers and 3 male.

The characters we see most briefly are viewed through the eye of the character who describes them. They should be larger than life and as such it is not necessary to cast according to gender or casting type.

Various doubling options are possible. For minimum sized cast the following doubling can work. .

MATT

SOPHIA

TASH

YAS/AWKWARD BOB/EMILY

HAYLEY/TASH'S MUM/HANNAH

CHLOE/MATT'S MUM/PSYCHIATRIST/LYDIA/LILLY

CHLOE'S MUM/PANDORA/ANNA

BIG BARRY/ DR. SILVERBERG/TAMMY/PARAMEDIC 1

DIRTY DAN/ SOPHIA'S DAD/FLORENCE/PARAMEDIC 2

Characters

MATT

SOPHIA

TASH

EMILY

LILLY

HANNAH

ANNA

PANDORA

TAMMY

LYDIA

FLORENCE

SOPHIA'S DAD

DR. SILVERBERG

BIG BARRY

DIRTY DAN

AWKWARD BOB

HAYLEY

CHLOE

MATT'S MUM

YAS

TASH'S MUM

CHLOE'S MUM

PARAMEDIC 1

PARAMEDIC 2

PSYCHIATRIST

PROLOGUE

The cast bursts onto the stage. Music plays. We are at a festival. Everyone is happy, laughing and dancing. From the crowd **TASH**, **SOPHIA** *and* **MATT** *talk to the audience.*

TASH: Summer.

MATT: Exams are over.

SOPHIA: Finally.

TASH: And results are months away.

SOPHIA: Do I know you?

MATT: Not yet.

TASH: I just thought you seemed…?

SOPHIA: Familiar?

MATT: *(Back to the audience.)* We don't go to the same school.

SOPHIA: We don't know the same people.

TASH: We've never met before.

SOPHIA: But today we're going to meet.

MATT: We'll pass each other in the crowd.

TASH: And we'll smile.

MATT: Because we like the same music.

TASH: Because the sun is shining.

SOPHIA: Because we're at a festival and there's no reason not to smile.

MATT: Time to relax.

SOPHIA: Time to breathe out for the first time in a long time.

TASH: Time for the long summer after GCSEs.

MATT: And I'm excited cause we managed to get tickets.

SOPHIA: And I'm excited cause my parents said yes.

TASH: And I'm excited 'cause it's three whole days of music

SOPHIA: And dancing.

MATT: Just me and my mates in a field somewhere covered in mud.

TASH: And it's like all my worries are melting into the mud

MATT: And it's like everything that happened is being carried away on the wind.

SOPHIA: And I'm not *that* person…

TASH: *That* girl

MATT: *That* boy

SOPHIA: *That* attention seeking girl I'm just

TASH: Tash

SOPHIA: Sophia

MATT: Matt

SOPHIA: Three completely different people

MATT: Three completely different journeys

TASH: Three completely different stories

SOPHIA: At one completely brilliant festival.

MATT: So…shall I…?

SOPHIA: Yeah go on.

MATT: *(Clears throat.)* Matt, Sophia and Tash present…

ALL: Hidden.

TASH: It's a play.

MATT: It's about…well it's about us.

SOPHIA: It's about self-worth

MATT: Mental health

SOPHIA: And self-harm.

TASH: 'Cause we need to work out where it started.

SOPHIA: We need to go back to the beginning.

MATT: Way back

TASH: To the first time I did it.

SOPHIA: Before then.

MATT: Way before.

SOPHIA: So it can all start to make sense.

SCENE 1

MATT: So I'm in year 9 and I don't have a care in the world. I've got great mates.

(As each character is introduced they appear.)

MATT: There's Big Barry. Baz. No one messes with him but he's a teddy bear when you get to know 'im. Dirty Dan.

DAN: Oh my God, I was with that girl right and we were doing it and she was screaming my name mate and…

MATT: Total virgin. And awkward Bob.

*(**MATT** tries to fist bump awkward **BOB** and fails.)*

MATT: And we're hanging around with Hayley Chapman and…

*(At this point **BOB** awkwardly goes and stands far too close to **HAYLEY**.)*

MATT: Bob. Bob mate. Give the girl some breathing space.

*(**BOB** does not move.)*

MATT: Bob. Seriously. Be cool.

*(**BOB** awkwardly moves away but keeps staring at **HAYLEY**.)*

MATT: Hayley has that effect on guys. She's so fit but it's like she doesn't even know. None of us can work out why she even hangs around with us but we're all totally chuffed that she does. Oh and her mate Chloe completes the set.

*(**CHLOE** enters. No one much notices.)*

SCENE 2

Thorpe Park.

MATT: It's summer term and it's activity week and somehow the business studies teacher has managed to blag that we're going to Thorpe Park. As a business trip! I'm definitely going to take business studies now.

HAYLEY: Me too.

BARRY: Yeah and me.

DAN: *(Throwing his arms intrusively around **CHLOE** and **HAYLEY**.)* Well if you girls are taking it then I guess I'll have to rethink my options.

MATT: Stop being such a slime ball.

DAN: Just sayin' that's all.

CHLOE: You're seriously going to decide your whole future based on a trip which is a cynical bribe to make you think taking business studies is going to mean hanging about with your mates and going on roller coasters.

MATT: Yep.

HAYLEY: Pretty much.

BARRY: Works for me.

DAN: I don't see the problem sweetheart.

*(**BOB** has not answered. Everyone is waiting for him to speak.)*

MATT: Bob. Mate. What about you?

BOB: What?

MATT: You gonna take business studies next year?

BOB: No. I'm taking textiles.

BARRY: Textiles?

BOB: Yeah.

CHLOE: Good for you Bob. You follow that dream.

DAN: But textiles?!!!!

MATT: So we get on the minibus and we all squeeze into the back seat and I can feel Hayley's leg brushing up against mine

ALL: And we are off.

HAYLEY: And Dan's telling some totally crap story about this girl he met on holiday.

(We see this story told through the power of gesture.)

MATT: And I'm thinking she's sitting really close. I hope I don't smell bad. I did spray but did I spray enough and I try to subtly sniff my pits.

CHLOE: What's Matt doing. Is he hiding?

HAYLEY: And someone on this bus has sprayed far too much and it's giving me a headache. *(To **MATT**.)* Can you smell that?

MATT: What?

HAYLEY: It smells like a cross between blocked up drains and candy floss. It's gross. Can you really not smell that?

MATT: Oh that? Yeah, I can smell that.

HAYLEY: Totally gross.

MATT: Horrible.

*(**MATT** tries unsuccessfully to neutralise his pits by rubbing them.)*

BARRY: And Chloe's re-doing her make up again.

HAYLEY: And Matt keeps scratching himself. I hope he hasn't got ringworm.

DAN: And Barry tries unsuccessfully to start a singsong.

*(**BARRY** fails to start a singsong.)*

HAYLEY: Or scabies.

CHLOE: And Dan keeps trying to put his arm around me.

HAYLEY: Or fleas.

CHLOE: And then two minutes before we reach our destination Bob chunders.

ALL: Ewww. Oh Bob. Did you have to? Mate!

MATT: And finally we're there.

HAYLEY: And it's raining a bit but we don't care.

DAN: We don't even have to queue.

BARRY: 'Cause all those other suckers are still chained to their desks.

CHLOE: And Sir's going over some ground rules and expectations…

HAYLEY: But we're not really listening 'cause…

BARRY: We can smell the hot dogs.

DAN: We can hear the music…

HAYLEY: And the people screaming so…

ALL: We are off.

DAN: And we all go on all the roller coasters

BARRY: And the pirate boat

CHLOE: And the magic carpet

MATT: And even the kiddie rides 'cause well why not

HAYLEY: And then we get on the log flume.

(They are now on the log flume.)

DAN: I mean this is just pathetic. I mean I've taken my three-year-old cousin on scarier rides. There was this one time we were in Portugal right and their rides are much scarier than this and..

*(**DAN** is taken by surprise by a sudden dip.)*

ALL: *(Especially **DAN**.)*
AAAAAAAAAAAAAAAAAAAAHHHHHHHHHHH!

MATT: And we're completely soaked.

HAYLEY: Except for Bob.

*(To the others' incredulity, **BOB** is completely dry. Maybe he had a hidden poncho, mac or umbrella.)*

CHLOE: And we go and get a coffee to warm ourselves up.

HAYLEY: And Chloe disappears to sort out her make-up.

BARRY: She looks like a very sad clown.

MATT: And Dan and Barry skulk off too for a sneaky fag.

HAYLEY: Leaving just me and Matt.

MATT: And Bob.

BARRY: *(Sticking his head around the door.)* Bob mate you coming?

BOB: I'm alright mate.

DAN: Bob. *(Pointedly and unsubtle.)* We need to talk to you!

BARRY: Seriously it's urgent.

BOB: But I want to get a soya, decaf mocha latte.

*(**BIG BARRY** and **DIRTY DAN** physically remove **BOB** from the scene.)*

SCENE 3

MATT: So it's just Hayley and me. *(To **HAYLEY**.)* Pretty wet.

HAYLEY: Yep. I bet I look like a drowned rat.

MATT: No you look fine.

HAYLEY: Fine?

MATT: Alright you look nice.

HAYLEY: Nice. That the best you got?

MATT: Sorry I mean you look, you look really nice...lovely?

*(**HAYLEY** is laughing.)*

HAYLEY: I'm only mucking about.

MATT: Yeah, sure. I know. Me too.

*(**MATT** takes his wet hoodie off. He has a T shirt underneath.)*

HAYLEY: My jeans are soaked.

MATT: My t shirt's actually not too bad. I think my hoodie took the worst of it. Feel.

(He places her hand on his chest. Beat.)

MATT: Do you want to take yours off? We're right by a radiator they should dry...

HAYLEY: No. I'm alright.

MATT: Are you sure, 'cause you'll catch your death.

HAYLEY: I can't.

MATT: What?

HAYLEY: I can't take it off. I don't like my arms.

MATT: *(Laughing)* What?

HAYLEY: Don't laugh. They're chunky.

MATT: They are not. Don't be ridiculous. Give me your hoodie and I'll put it by the radiator to dry.

*(**HAYLEY** considers it for a moment and then slowly takes off her hoodie. Underneath she wears a T shirt and her now exposed arms are covered in scars.)*

MATT: See I told you you're not chunk...

(Silence.)

And it's then I see them. Lots and lots of scars on the top of her arms. Some of them must have been from a long time ago 'cause they're faded now but some seem sort of fresh. And I want to look at them, hell I want to kiss them all better, but I also want to run far, far away.

And it's like time is standing still and she knows I've seen but haven't said anything and every second I'm standing here is a second I feel her ebbing away from me and I hear myself say, 'Do you want to talk about it?' And she starts to cry.

HAYLEY: And I'm telling him everything. It's all tumbling out in a complete mess and I'm totally mortified because I hate crying in front of people…and we're not talking about a few artistically placed teardrops…I'm talking about proper bawling ugly crying…

MATT: And she is telling me all of it, about her new step-dad's kids and the rows with her mum and, even though she's crying a lot, she still looks beautiful…

HAYLEY: And I'm thinking he must be really embarrassed because everyone in the coffee shop must have noticed…

MATT: And it's like everyone in the coffee shop has faded away and it's just me and Hayley.

HAYLEY: And I don't know why I'm telling him all this.

MATT: And I don't know why she's telling me all this but I'm weirdly pleased she likes me enough to tell me so I reach out…

HAYLEY: And he holds my hand.

MATT: And her hand feels so small and I just want to protect her and I don't want to let go so…

HAYLEY: He starts asking me questions.

MATT: I ask her how long she's been doing it.

HAYLEY: And I tell him it's almost a year now and he doesn't seem shocked…

MATT: And I'm shocked. Why on earth would a girl like that. A popular, pretty, smart girl like that do something so… dark…

HAYLEY: And I like that he doesn't seem shocked or disgusted and that he seems to accept it…

MATT: And I like it. I like this. I like that she's telling me. I like that she's not as perfect as I thought she was. That she's showing me this part she's kept hidden. That she's letting me in.

HAYLEY: And I'm thinking maybe this isn't so weird. Sat here right now, holding Matt's hand I'm thinking maybe I'm not so weird after all…

MATT: And I ask her how often she does it, what she uses and why.

HAYLEY: And, as I tell him, I tell him all of it, it's like a weight is lifted from me. And he's telling me I have to stop and I'm agreeing and nodding.

MATT: And, as I'm telling her she has to stop, I can't stop the pictures she is painting from flashing through my head and I know whilst…

HAYLEY: He tells me I'm beautiful and shouldn't hurt myself

MATT: That she's put the idea in my head and…

HAYLEY: He tells me that he'll keep my secret and help me to stop.

MATT: But my interest is piqued.

HAYLEY: That I'm relieved to have told someone.

MATT: That I'm honoured to have been told.

DAN: Got any toothpaste?

MATT: And I'm slinging my damp hoodie over her shoulders.

HAYLEY: What?

BARRY: Sir might have seen us having a fag.

DAN: Chewing gum?

HAYLEY: Err yeah, I think so.

MATT: And she's letting go of my hand.

HAYLEY: And the moment has gone. And we're heading out again.

MATT: And she's mouthing thank you to me.

HAYLEY: And we don't talk about it again for almost a year.

MATT: And I don't think about it again for whole six months.

SCENE 4

TASH: So you started doing it because of some girl you fancied?

MATT: Not straight away. But yeah, if I'm honest that's where I got the idea.

SOPHIA: But you told her not to do it?

MATT: I know.

SOPHIA: But you still went on to do it yourself?

MATT: Yeah.

TASH: That doesn't make sense.

MATT: I know.

TASH: *(To* **SOPHIA**.*)* Okay. Well what about you? What made you start?

SOPHIA: I think for me the signs were there way earlier. Maybe even in primary school.

SCENE 5

Flashback. **SOPHIA** *is aged seven with her friends.*

HANNAH: My mum said we could have the sleepover at ours.

SOPHIA: Are you serious?

HANNAH: Yeah, she said we can have our sleeping bags in the living room and watch DVDs and eat popcorn and ice cream and she even said she'll let us do our nails…

ANNA: I want pink.

EMILY: Can I have purple?

LILLY: Can I have purple too.

EMILY: No. You can have lilac. I'm having purple.

HANNAH: The thing is 'cause we've got the builders in Mum says that there isn't really enough room to have everyone to stay at the same time. But she said we can do it twice and have two of you this weekend and two in a couple of weekends' time.

SOPHIA: But I thought we'd all be together.

HANNAH: Yeah but we can't 'cause of the builders. So this weekend I'll have Anna and Emily. Then next time you and Lilly can come.

SOPHIA: Oh right. Okay. I just…I didn't realise…

SOPHIA *begins to cry uncontrollably.*

HANNAH: Oh Sophia don't cry.

EMILY: Not again.

HANNAH: We will have a sleepover just not yet.

SOPHIA: No, I know, it's fine. I just thought we would be all together that's all.

HANNAH: It's okay. Do you want a hug?

EMILY: Look Sophia. Do you see Lilly crying?

ANNA: She's just upset.

EMILY: She's being really immature. Lilly's going to the later sleepover too and she's not crying.

ANNA: Do you want to go in my place Sophia? I don't mind swapping.

HANNAH: Yeah, how about that?

EMILY: But that's not fair. Hannah chose already. What about Lilly? She doesn't get to swap just cause she's not the one who's crying like a baby.

LILLY: Well what if we both swap and Sophia and me do this weekend and you and Anna do the later one.

EMILY: I don't see why we all have to change our plans just cause Sophia can't stop crying.

HANNAH: But she's upset.

EMILY: But she always does this. Whatever it is we have to ruin it with Sophia crying and getting everyone's attention. She does this all the time.

SOPHIA: I'm sorry, I just can't… I'm sorry

SOPHIA *runs off.*

HANNAH: Look what you made her do!

SCENE 6

MATT: You really think the signs were there all that time ago?

TASH: 'Cause you were a bit of a cry baby?

SOPHIA: You don't get it. I know that was just a minor, nothingy thing but to me it really mattered. It hurt.

TASH: If you say so.

SOPHIA: I just found it really hard to regulate my emotions. When I was up I was really up but when I'd feel down I just couldn't calm myself down.

TASH: But that was nothing.

MATT: How do you decide?

TASH: What?

MATT: What counts as a real problem. That was real to Sophia.

TASH: Yeah but it obviously wasn't really…

MATT: But it felt real.

SOPHIA: Come on then spill the beans. What made you embark on this voyage of self-destruction.

SCENE 7

TASH: I was never really very good at talking to people. I mainly existed at the edge of things. I kept my head down, did my schoolwork, tried to make sure I didn't draw attention to myself. I didn't have friends, but I wasn't bullied. No one was deliberately cruel. I wasn't anything. I was just not really there. Then in year 9 Yas arrived.

(YAS enters.)

TASH: She rocked up at school in the middle of a term. Didn't know anybody. Hip in a Hijab and she acted like, I dunno, like she belonged there. She'd just walk down the corridor, shoulders back, head held high and, when she passed you, she'd smile at you. And I was put with her in science and she'd just chat to me, easy as anything. And she actually seemed to like me. Soon, pretty soon, the whole school knew her name and she was form rep and part of the debating team and she played netball. And I couldn't believe it. She'd chosen me as a friend and acted like it was no big deal. I thought nothing could touch her and then one day I found her in the girls' toilets.

SCENE 8

YAS is in the loos.

YAS is upset trying to fix her head scarf.

TASH: Yas. Yas. Are you okay?

YAS: They just make me sick.

TASH: Who? Yas, what's happened?

YAS: They have no right. No right at all.

TASH: Who? Talk to me Yas.

YAS: Lucy and her pathetic friends in year 11.

TASH: What did they do?

YAS: No right whatsoever. Argh. I'm just so angry.

TASH: Do you want me to get someone?

YAS: No.

TASH: Are you hurt?

YAS: No.

TASH: What do you want me to do Yas?

YAS: Don't get someone.

TASH: But if they're picking on you…

YAS: You have absolutely no idea do you? You haven't got the faintest clue…?

TASH: What?

YAS: This is just how it is. They can say whatever they like to me and I'm expected to just take it. Be a good little meek Muslim girl. Well I'm sick of it.

TASH: What did they say?

YAS: Nothing I haven't heard before.

TASH: Please just tell me what happened? And she's telling me. She's telling me all of it and I've never seen her so angry. She's telling me how she was walking down the corridor and

YAS: Suddenly Lucy was there with the others. They kept talking about my rucksack. Saying everyone needs to be careful because I might be a suicide bomber who's lost her way

TASH: And I'm telling her that's ridiculous but it's like she can't even hear me she's so incandescent with rage.

YAS: Something sort of pinged in my brain so I told them that not every Muslim is some kind of terrorist but they started pulling at my rucksack and getting really rough.

TASH: And she's so angry now that she can barely spit out of her words.

YAS: Somehow my head scarf got caught and got ripped clean off my head.

TASH: And she's crying now and telling me she feels exposed and stupid and angry and ashamed. And I don't know what to say. I can't imagine what she must be feeling. So I'm just hugging her and I want to be telling her that I understand and that it will all be alright but I don't understand and it won't be alright.

So, I'm just hugging her and I want to be telling her that I understand and that it will all be alright but I don't understand and it won't be alright so…

YAS *is calming down and dabbing her eyes.*

TASH: *(Tentatively.)* Yas. We need to tell someone.

YAS: Oh. Do we?

TASH: They can't be allowed to get away with that.

YAS: Just leave it.

TASH: I'm serious.

YAS: I can handle it.

TASH: What if they pick on someone who can't handle it next time? Someone could get really upset or really hurt. Please Yas. Just come with me and we'll…

YAS: I said leave it.

SCENE 9

SOPHIA: And did you leave it?

TASH: Yeah…she didn't want me to say anything.

MATT: But that's a serious thing she's talking about. Someone could have got really hurt. She needed help.

TASH: I realise that now.

SOPHIA: You can't force someone to get help.

TASH: No. Not if they're not ready.

MATT: You thought that if you kept her secret it would show her she could trust you.

TASH: Exactly.

MATT: Same reason I didn't say anything about Hayley.

SOPHIA: No one wants to be the one to tell.

MATT: But then you realise if you don't do something, tell someone, nothing's going to change. That's why I finally decided to tell my mum. She'd always been there for me so…

TASH: And…?

MATT: Well it wasn't easy.

SCENE 10

MATT's *house.*

MATT'S MUM: Oh Matt, thank goodness you're home. That computer's on the blink again. The screen won't come on. Do you think it's that router?

MATT: I doubt it if the screen…

MATT'S MUM: I was just trying to get that dolly off your cousin's wish list. She'll be seven on Monday? Seven! Can't believe it. Seems like it was only yesterday that we were going to visit her up St Peters. Do you remember love?

MATT: Mum, can we…?

MATT'S MUM: You were only seven or eight at the time. Do you remember?

MATT: Can we talk?

MATT'S MUM: You had that ridiculous Ben Ten watch that kept beeping the whole time and you barely even looked at Abby and when Zita asked you what you thought of the baby do you remember what you said?

MATT: Mum?

MATT'S MUM: You said, 'she doesn't do much does she?' And you did this adorable sulky little face. And we couldn't stop laughing. Zita almost burst her stitches. It's just the little arrow thing doesn't move about when you wiggle the thingymagig. Can you have a look love? It's driving me spare…

MATT: Mum!!!

MATT'S MUM: There's no need to shout. I'm sure there's a perfectly…

> **MATT** *takes off his hoodie revealing cuts on his upper arms.* **MUM** *stops in her tracks.*

MATT'S MUM: Well how did you…?

> **MATT** *is very upset.*

MATT: I'm sorry Mum.

MATT'S MUM: Oh Matt.

She abandons what she is doing and envelops him as he sobs.

MATT: I'm sorry.

MATT'S MUM: Don't be sorry.

MATT: Sorry.

MATT'S MUM: No sorry okay? There's no need to be sorry. I'm here. We can sort this out. It's okay. It's going to be okay.

SCENE 11

TASH: Wow.

SOPHIA: I didn't expect that did you?

TASH: No I thought she'd be cross with him.

SOPHIA: Or she'd just try and pretend it wasn't happening.

TASH: I thought she'd go ballistic.

MATT: *(Now having composed himself a little.)* Yeah me too.

TASH: I wish my mum had been like that.

SOPHIA: She was lovely.

MATT: Yeah. We sat down and talked. Well I talked. She mainly listened. She made me realise that although what I was doing made me feel better at the time, the feeling didn't last and then I'd just feel worse. I was stuck in this horrible cycle. She convinced me to go to the doctor and then he referred me to an expert.

TASH: And what did they do?

MATT: Wait. Hang on a minute…We're not even supposed to be in my story.

SOPHIA: Oh yeah. We asked you what made you start doing it and you just told us a story about your friend Yas.

MATT: Deflecting attention.

TASH: It was relevant.

SOPHIA: How?

MATT: This isn't meant to be Yas' story. It's yours.

TASH: She was the first person who knew about me.

MATT: You told her?

TASH: Not exactly.

SCENE 12

YAS: What's that on your arm?

TASH: It's nothing. I caught it on the hob.

YAS: Let me see. Tasha. What have you done to yourself? Let me…

She grabs **TASH**'s *sleeve and pulls it up.*

YAS: Tash. There's loads of marks here.

TASH: Please don't tell everyone.

YAS: What happened?

TASH: Just let it go.

YAS: Who did this to you?

TASH: It's not a big deal. Look you've got enough on your plate okay?

YAS: It's not okay. Is it your Mum…?

TASH: No.

YAS: 'Cause I could go with you and we could tell someone…?

TASH: It's not my Mum.

YAS: Is it someone at school?

TASH: No.

YAS: 'Cause if it is I promise you I'm gonna make it so their life isn't worth living…

TASH: It's nothing to do with school.

YAS: Then what is it to do with?

TASH: You wouldn't get it.

YAS: Try me.

TASH: Look this is stupid. I've told you I'm fine.

YAS: Look, you've got all these scars on your arm and you won't let me do anything about it and you won't tell me anything about it…what do you expect me to…

TASH: Do you promise not to tell anyone?

YAS: What?

TASH: You have to promise that if I tell you, you won't tell anyone. You'll keep it a secret.

YAS: But…

TASH: Please Yas. Just don't tell okay?

YAS: Okay. Okay. I won't tell.

TASH: Promise.

YAS: Yes, I promise. What happened Tash? Who hurt you?

TASH: I did. I did it myself.

YAS: You? What? Why?

TASH: I dunno. I've been doing it for a while.

YAS: That is seriously twisted.

TASH: Thanks.

YAS: No, sorry… I mean you don't need to do that to be cool or whatever…

TASH: What?

YAS: If you're doing it as some kind of fashion statement?

TASH: Are you actually serious?

YAS: Or you think people will pay more attention to you.

TASH: Oh wow. Right. Look just like not everyone who wears a head scarf is a terrorist not everyone who self-harms is doing it to be cool or for attention. I knew you wouldn't get it.

YAS: Oh I get it, 'you just felt like it.' What if you just felt like stealing a car and driving it off a bridge or you just felt like going into Mr. Donohue's office and stabbing him to death or you just felt like taking so many pills you didn't wake up.

TASH: You're just being stupid. Of course I'm not going to do anything that extreme.

YAS: This is extreme.

TASH: Lots of people do it.

YAS: Yes and lots of people do extreme things. That doesn't make it okay Tash.

TASH: Look. It's not a big deal. It's not something I'm going to do forever. It just makes me feel better sometimes. It's not really anyone else's business so…

YAS: I'm your friend. Of course it's my business. You may not be burning my arms but you're still hurting me Tash.

TASH: Well that makes me feel great.

YAS: Look. It hurts me to know that you are in that much pain that you need to do… that. That hurts me.

TASH: I said you wouldn't get it.

YAS: Okay, you're right. I don't get it. I don't get why someone as funny and talented and intelligent and beautiful as you would want to do that to themselves. I don't. Okay.

Silence.

YAS: Look Tasha. You need to get some help with this, you can't go on…

TASH: You promised.

YAS: What?

TASH: You said.

YAS: Yeah but…

TASH: You promised that you wouldn't tell anyone.

YAS: But I didn't know what it was…

TASH: It doesn't matter. You promised and if our friendship means anything to you…

YAS: You know it does.

TASH: Then keep your promise. That what friends do.

YAS: But Tash.

TASH: I said leave it.

SCENE 13

MATT: So that was it. You kept her secret so she kept yours.

TASH: Pretty much

SOPHIA: That's not really very healthy.

TASH: Yeah …It's just she was my only friend and I didn't want to lose her.

SOPHIA: At least you had friends.

TASH: What happened to all those girls you used to hang around with?

SOPHIA: Boarding school happened. That school went right through to 13. Then we'd take a whole bunch of exams and that decided what school we went to next and pretty much everyone went away to school.

MATT: Was it like in Harry Potter?

SOPHIA: Err no.

TASH: Shh.

MATT: I was just asking.

SOPHIA: Well it wasn't. Not for me. So me and Emily ended up both going to the same all girls boarding school.

MATT: Which one's Emily?

TASH: Let me guess she's the cow who kept calling you a cry baby right?

SOPHIA: Yeah.

TASH: Knew it.

SOPHIA: She wasn't that bad really. She just never really understood why I was so sensitive. I was still pleased to have someone I knew coming to my new school with me. So in our first year...

TASH: That's year 9 then.

SOPHIA: Yeah. They put us in the same dorm because we'd come from the same prep school. There were six of us in there. Me and Emily.

EMILY *appears.*

SOPHIA: And these four other girls who all knew each other from before.

As she introduces each character they appear/emerge/transform.

SOPHIA: So there's this girl Tammy who's completely obsessed with horses.

The actor playing **TAMMY** *pretends to ride about on a horse.* **SOPHIA** *looks pitying at them.*

SOPHIA: What are you doing?

ACTOR PLAYING TAMMY: I'm being the horsey girl.

SOPHIA: You look ridiculous. We are almost fourteen now not seven.

ACTOR PLAYING TAMMY: Right. Too much?

SOPHIA: Way too much.

The actor tones down their horsey acting. **SOPHIA** *looks at them pityingly.*

ACTOR PLAYING TAMMY: Well it's all you've given me to work with. Go on to the next one.

SOPHIA: This girl Florence who's like mega super brainy and Lydia who's really into Ballet.

FLORENCE and LYDIA appear.

SOPHIA: And Pandora. She's got this really long silky hair and when she moves her head it looks like a shampoo commercial. Everyone likes her. It's only the first day and already she's probably the most popular girl in school.

TASH: I hate her already.

SOPHIA: Shh. So it's the first day and everyone's settling in to the dorm room.

SCENE 14

PANDORA: Oh my God. This is a total disaster.

LYDIA: What's the matter?

PANDORA: No, no. It's okay.

FLORENCE: What's up?

PANDORA: It doesn't matter but like oh my God.

TAMMY: Tell us what's wrong.

PANDORA: You promise not to laugh?

The girls nod solemnly. They all gather in and PANDORA whispers. EMILY and SOPHIA sit awkwardly. Suddenly the girls are all staring over at SOPHIA.

LYDIA: Just ask her.

FLORENCE: I'm sure she won't mind.

TAMMY: It's not like she's unpacked.

FLORENCE: We've only just got here.

PANDORA: But I'm really embarrassed.

TAMMY: I'll do it if you like.

PANDORA: No. No. That's wouldn't be fair.

FLORENCE: We could all go?

PANDORA: It's okay. I can do it.

PANDORA *strides over to* **SOPHIA.**

PANDORA: Hi. I'm Pandora.

SOPHIA: I'm Sophia.

PANDORA: Right yeah. Hi. Erm the thing is. And I feel really awful saying this because it's really embarrassing but I've like got this thing.

SOPHIA: Okay.

PANDORA: It's like wherever I sleep I have to be by a window or I get like really claustrophobic and have nightmares and stuff.

SOPHIA: You want to swap beds?

PANDORA: Would that be okay?

SOPHIA: Yeah sure. No problem.

PANDORA: Really? That's so kind of you.

SOPHIA: That's okay. It makes no difference to me and if you're going to feel more comfortable.

PANDORA: I really will.

SOPHIA: Okay. Let me just move my stuff.

From under the pillow **SOPHIA** *removes her pyjamas and picks up her bag to move.*

PANDORA: Erm. Did you like already put your stuff in the bed?

SOPHIA: It's okay. I don't mind moving it.

PANDORA: No. Look you've already practically unpacked so…

SOPHIA: It's really not a big deal.

PANDORA: So let's just stick with what we've got okay?

SOPHIA: It really is fine. I'll just go over there…

PANDORA: Look. I don't really feel comfortable sleeping in a bed where your under things have been under my pillow.

SOPHIA: It's my pyjamas and they're clean.

PANDORA: Yeah, yeah, I know. It's just me being weird. I'll just go to the other bed. Thanks and everything but I'd feel more comfortable.

PANDORA goes back to the empty bed dejectedly.

SOPHIA: We could always swap the bed sheets over?

PANDORA: What?

SOPHIA: I could move my bed sheets over there and you could bring yours over here?

PANDORA: You'd be willing to do that?

SOPHIA: Yeah, sure. If you'll feel more comfortable?

PANDORA: Yeah. I really think I would.

SOPHIA: Okay. Lets do it.

SOPHIA starts to swap the bed sheets.

PANDORA: That's great. Thank you so much.

SOPHIA: No problem.

PANDORA: Oh actually there's that meet and greet with the house parents in the common room now. Would you mind meeting us down there? I don't want to be late and make a bad impression.

SOPHIA: Erm. Maybe I could come too and do this later?

PANDORA: I'd really rather not come back to an unmade bed. I mean you're almost done.

SOPHIA: Sure. Okay. See you down there.

The girls have gone. **EMILY** *hesitates then follows them.*

SCENE 15

TASH: What a complete piece of work.

MATT: Why didn't you stand up to her?

SOPHIA: It wasn't that easy. She didn't actually seem to be doing anything wrong. Whenever I talked to a teacher about it they'd say it was just girls being girls and six of one and half a dozen of the other.

TASH: Typical. Anyone with half a brain could see what she was.

SOPHIA: I couldn't. I thought she was my friend.

MATT: Seriously?

SOPHIA: Yeah. I think she thought she was as well.

TASH: How could she possibly…?

SOPHIA: Look boarding school's a bit weird okay. Lots of people really like it but, if you're like me, and you find it hard, there's no escape. You can't get away from the people who are making you feel bad. They're with you 24/7. I had no way to get away and they just made me feel like I was different, the odd one out…less than they were.

MATT: Makes you think don't it.

TASH: What?

MATT: You never know what's going on inside someone's head. Even a rich little daddy's girl…

SOPHIA: I'm not a daddy's girl.

TASH: You've got a job then?

SOPHIA: Well no.

TASH: Who paid for your ticket?

SOPHIA: Well my parents but…

TASH: And you went to a fee paying school?

SOPHIA: Yeah but…

TASH: Got a pony?

SOPHIA: Well no actually 'cause my dad sold it cause I never rode it so…

> **TASH** and **MATT** *both laugh.*

SOPHIA: Look it's not funny.

MATT: It is a bit funny.

SOPHIA: Having money doesn't make you immune to mental health problems. One in four people experience a mental health problem at some point in their lives okay? It's not one in four poor people.

MATT: Okay sorry your highness. Us mere peasants…

SOPHIA: Not one in four people on benefits…

TASH: Oh me lady can you spare us some change?

SOPHIA: If you're going to be like that I won't tell you anymore.

MATT: Oh come on we're only joking.

TASH: It's just a bit of banter.

SOPHIA: Well I don't think it's very funny. Why are we even talking about me? We're supposed to be in Tash's story.

MATT: You've done it again.

TASH: What?

SOPHIA: You don't have to tell us. Not if you don't want to.

TASH: No. It's okay. I'm okay about it now that I've talked things through with a professional. It's just a bit of a difficult story for other people to hear.

MATT: It's okay.

SOPHIA: We want to hear it.

SCENE 16

TASH: So before I was four, I don't really remember much. I know it was just me and Mum. I've never known my dad and I don't think we had much money but, other than that, things were fine. We got on with it.

Then when I was about four, Mum met Andy. I really liked him and I was happy because she was happy and I remember he'd bring ice cream and books and stuff. Pretty soon he was staying over every night so, when Mum asked if I'd mind if he came to live with us permanently, it didn't seem like that much of a big deal. I liked him. I even asked if I could call him Dad and he laughed and agreed.

I don't remember much because I was so little. I remember sitting on his lap and him brushing my hair for hours. I remember him lying next to me in bed when I was ill and couldn't get to sleep.

Then when I was seven, I can remember this one thing. I remember Mum coming into my room when he was there and getting really angry. She just kept shouting and shouting at him and telling him she'd call the police and he kept crying and saying he wouldn't do it again and I was just yelling and yelling at them to stop shouting.

The next morning, he was gone, and Mum told me that if he came to the house I mustn't go to the door and if he rang the house phone I should hang up.

I asked her why, but she just kept crying and saying she was sorry and telling me to eat my cereal.

She didn't say it but I always thought it was my fault that Andy left. I don't know why but I felt like I'd stopped my mum from having her greatest chance of happiness. We moved soon after that and I never saw him again.

SCENE 17

SOPHIA: He was abusing you?

TASH: Yeah.

MATT: Sick pervert.

SOPHIA: I'm so sorry.

TASH: Don't be sorry for me. Be sorry for my mum. I didn't even know what was happening.

SOPHIA: But still. That's rough. I mean no wonder you ended up…

TASH: Really? You think it seems like an obvious link? Kid gets abused by her step-dad and obviously goes on to self-harm?

SOPHIA: Well no, not necessarily but there must be something…

TASH: Lots of people go through far worse.

SOPHIA: Yeah but it's not really surprising it would affect your self-esteem.

MATT: Especially if you thought all this time you'd done something wrong.

TASH: I don't even remember it.

SOPHIA: I suppose that doesn't matter.

TASH: You sound like my psychiatrist.

MATT: So your psychiatrist helped you work things out?

TASH: Eventually but now you're skipping ahead. I don't get to meet her for another seven years. What about you guys? Any horrible and disturbing skeletons in the closet whilst we're all up for sharing and caring?

MATT: No.

SOPHIA: Nothing like that.

TASH: So not everyone who self-harms has a screwed up abusive childhood.

MATT: Nope.

TASH: Guess I'm just lucky. Come on then Princess what made you turn to the dark side?

MATT: Oh leave it out?

TASH: No come on. I'm curious.

SOPHIA: It seems really pathetic now.

TASH: It obviously mattered to you though.

SOPHIA: Well yeah but compared to what you've just said. I just feel …

MATT: Just tell us.

TASH: It must have been pretty bad if you ended up…well what did you end up doing?

SOPHIA: Okay. So I didn't really settle at boarding school and the more I tried to fit in the more out of it I felt. So there was this one day and everyone else had gone swimming but I was back at the dorm because I had period pains.

MATT: Eww.

TASH: Get over it.

SOPHIA: And Emily came to check up on me.

SCENE 18

SOPHIA's *dorm.*

EMILY: Hey Soph. Sophia. You awake?

SOPHIA: Yeah.

EMILY: You okay?

SOPHIA: Yeah. I've just got stomach-ache that's all.

EMILY: Time of the month?

SOPHIA: Yeah.

EMILY: That sucks.

SOPHIA: Yep.

EMILY: I'm really lucky. Mine hardly hurt at all.

SOPHIA: Good for you.

EMILY: Sorry. I didn't mean to be insensitive. I just wanted to check you were okay.

SOPHIA: I know. Sorry. Yeah, I'm okay.

EMILY: So if you weren't feeling so rough you would go swimming with us?

SOPHIA: Yeah.

EMILY: Are you sure?

SOPHIA: Yeah, why not?

EMILY: It's just a few of us were wondering if, and you can tell me this is none of my business, we thought you might feel a bit, I don't know, self-conscious in a swimsuit.

SOPHIA: Why would you think that?

EMILY: I mean, we're not saying you should feel self-conscious or anything and it's really great if you don't cause we all think you're really pretty anyway…

SOPHIA: You think I'm pretty?

EMILY: Yeah, we all do. Pan was just saying the other day that you'd be like one of the prettiest girls here if you just lost a few pounds..

SOPHIA: So you are saying I'm fat?

EMILY: No, no, not fat. We'd never say that. Just you are little bit bigger than the rest of us so we just thought…

SOPHIA: Well don't okay?

EMILY: I didn't mean it like that. We just want to help. And I mean maybe, if you weren't so big then your period might not hurt as much.

SOPHIA: What?

EMILY: I dunno. I mean I'm not a doctor but none of the rest of us get this rough with it so I just wondered…

SOPHIA: Right.

EMILY: Oh Soph.

SOPHIA: Thanks a lot Emily.

EMILY: I just wanted to help.

SOPHIA: Well you're not helping.

EMILY: It's just that a few of us were feeling not fat but like we're a bit bigger than we want to be, so we've been taking these.

She produces some pills.

SOPHIA: What are they? Are they illegal?

EMILY: Don't be ridiculous. Pan bought them in Boots. They just help you shed a few extra pounds.

SOPHIA: How do they work.

EMILY: You just sort of poo it out.

SOPHIA: Delightful. And you've all been using them?

EMILY: Not all of us but me, Pan and Lydia have so…do you want to try?

SOPHIA: Yeah. Okay. Thanks Emily.

EMILY: No problem. Hope you feel better.

SOPHIA: Thanks.

SCENE 19

TASH: Oh God. That's horrible.

SOPHIA: I think she was trying to be helpful.

MATT: Really?

SOPHIA: Yeah. In her own way. I don't think she realised what she'd done.

MATT: What had she done?

SOPHIA: She'd planted the seed.

TASH: What do you mean?

SOPHIA: I was already feeling lonely and sad and like I was different from everyone else but then, when she gave me those pills…

TASH: Laxatives.

SOPHIA: Yeah.

TASH: They can be really dangerous.

SOPHIA: She made me think all my problems were because I looked different or I wasn't good looking enough. I started to think that if I looked better I'd feel better. And the thought kept just going round and around in my head. You're ugly.

MATT: You're not ugly.

SOPHIA: You're fat…

TASH: You're not…

SOPHIA: It doesn't matter how many times you're told you're not. It just keeps whirling around in your head. You're fat, you're ugly, nobody wants to be seen with you. I just couldn't shake that thought. Do you understand what I mean?

TASH: Yeah I do.

MATT: Me too.

SOPHIA: Really?

TASH: Completely.

MATT: Hi. I'm Matt and I used to think I was stupid.

TASH: Hi. I'm Tash. I used to think everyone would be happier if I wasn't here.

SOPHIA: Ouch.

TASH: But I don't think that any more.

SOPHIA: What made you change?

TASH: It took a really long time. But eventually I had to accept that I needed help so I agreed to see a psychiatrist.

SCENE 20

PSYCHIATRIST: Tash?

TASH: Yes.

MATT: That's your psychiatrist?

TASH: Yeah that's Lisa.

MATT: She's really young.

TASH: So?

MATT: I just imagined some old guy with a beard and a white coat.

TASH: Don't believe everything you see on TV.

MATT: I don't know. I just thought a psychiatrist would be some big scary…I mean she's hot!

SOPHIA: Matt!

MATT: Yeah sorry.

PSYCHIATRIST: Do you know why you've been sent to me?

TASH: I overdosed.

SOPHIA: You overdosed?

TASH: I told you things got worse before they got better.

MATT: Yeah but I didn't realise you'd…I just didn't know it had gone that far.

SOPHIA: I'm so sorry.

PSYCHIATRIST: And have you done this before?

TASH: I burned myself before but never this.

PSYCHIATRIST: Can you tell me what happened to trigger this latest incident?

TASH: My friend Yas. I thought I'd lost her.

PSYCHIATRIST: How did it make you feel?

TASH: Like everything would be better if it wasn't for me. If I'd only been a better friend or actually cared enough to ask her what was going on with her then maybe she wouldn't have…

PSYCHIATRIST: Okay. And when you've felt like this before how did you try to cope?

TASH: I'd talk to Yas. But Yas wasn't there so I felt worse

PSYCHIATRIST: So that's when you did it?

TASH: Yes.

PSYCHIATRIST: And how did that make you feel?

TASH: I felt better because I was stopping it. I was stopping myself from inflicting any more pain and suffering onto the people I love.

PSYCHIATRIST: And did that feeling last?

TASH: No! I felt dreadful listening to mum crying and talking to the doctors. I just made everything worse. On top of everything now she had to worry about me topping myself.

PSYCHIATRIST: And how did you feel?

TASH: Like everything would be better if it wasn't for me.

PSYCHIATRIST: So where do you want to break the cycle?

SCENE 21

SOPHIA: That's not how I imagined it.

TASH: In what way?

SOPHIA: Well she actually asked what you wanted.

TASH: Yeah, it took a while for me to work out what I did really want but Lisa helped me to do that.

SOPHIA: I thought, I dunno, when you think of a psychiatrist you imagine them telling you what to do.

TASH: Yeah I was surprised we didn't really talk about my self harming much at first just about everything around it. My mum had talked about pretty much nothing but my self harming for months so it was a nice break.

SOPHIA: At least your mum wanted to talk about it. My parents treated the whole thing like a massive inconvenience.

MATT: Did you try and talk to them?

SOPHIA: Even after school called them they just wanted to pretend that nothing was happening.

SCENE 22

SOPHIA'S DAD: Hello Pumpkin.

46

SOPHIA: Dad.

> **SOPHIA** *dissolves and sobs in her father's arms.*

SOPHIA'S DAD: Hey, hey. It's okay. I'm here. It's okay.

> **SOPHIA** *tries unsuccessfully to calm herself.*

SOPHIA'S DAD: Shh shh. It's okay. Take some deep breaths okay? Come one. With me. In and out. In and out. Okay?

> **SOPHIA** *calms down a little then blurts out.*

SOPHIA: It's just…

SOPHIA'S DAD: Calmly okay. Take a breath.

SOPHIA: Can I come home Dad?

SOPHIA'S DAD: What's this?

SOPHIA: I want to change schools.

SOPHIA'S DAD: We're not going to make any decisions at all whilst you're this upset okay?

SOPHIA: But I'm going to be upset while I'm here.

SOPHIA'S DAD: Look Miss Barton told me about your erm…the accident…and

> **SOPHIA** *sobs harder.*

SOPHIA'S DAD: Look, it's okay.

SOPHIA: It's not. Now no one wants to share a dorm with me next year.

SOPHIA'S DAD: Oh I'm sure that's not the case. She said everyone's been really mature and understanding…

SOPHIA: They're not.

SOPHIA'S DAD: Look, I know having diarrhoea is horrible but it could happen to anyone…people understand that.

SOPHIA: They don't.

SOPHIA'S DAD: Look I'm sure they do. And Miss Barton has said she's going to keep an extra close eye on you and she's made a referral for you to talk to a counsellor about erm...the other stuff..

SOPHIA: What other stuff?

SOPHIA'S DAD: She said you haven't been coping recently. Now you know we've been here before. Sometimes a new school and everything, it can just be a bit...overwhelming...

SOPHIA: What did she mean not coping?

SOPHIA'S DAD: Soph.

SOPHIA: What did she mean not coping!

SOPHIA'S DAD: She said one of the other girls...

SOPHIA: Who?

SOPHIA'S DAD: She didn't say just someone in your dorm had mentioned to her that they were concerned.

SOPHIA: Concerned about what?!

SOPHIA'S DAD: They said you've been pulling at your hair. Pulling bits out while you think no one's looking.

SOPHIA *self-consciously touches her hair and starts to cry.*

SOPHIA'S DAD: Pumpkin? Hey...hey look at me...why are you doing that?

SOPHIA: I'm not.

SOPHIA'S DAD: Pumpkin.

SOPHIA: Look I just want to come home with you. Can I come home with you Dad?

SOPHIA'S DAD: Look your mother and I have talked to Miss Barton and we all feel...

SOPHIA: What about what I feel?

SOPHIA'S DAD: We feel that it would be best for you to stay here where you can be kept a close eye on. You know if you come home you'll end up by yourself a lot of....

SOPHIA: I don't care.

SOPHIA'S DAD: We just think you'll be better here. You're settled here. You've got your friends…

SOPHIA: I haven't. No one wants to be in my dorm next year.

SOPHIA'S DAD: Now I'm sure that's not true.

SOPHIA: Where's Mum?

SOPHIA'S DAD: Look, you know she couldn't get away this time.

SOPHIA: I want to talk to Mum.

SOPHIA'S DAD: You can talk to her on the phone later but she's only going to say what I'm saying now. You need to stay at school, concentrate on your lessons, speak to the counsellor and in a week or two all this will have blown over. *(Pause.)* Okay?

SOPHIA *is still very upset but knows she is beaten.*

SOPHIA: *(Numbly.)* Okay.

SOPHIA'S DAD: Now give your old Dad a hug before I go.

SOPHIA *hugs him.*

SCENE 23

MATT: And he just left you there?

SOPHIA: He thought he was doing the right thing.

TASH: Yeah but he wasn't.

SOPHIA: He didn't realise how serious things were. He'd never heard of Trichotillomania.

MATT: What?

SOPHIA: It's a condition where a person feels compelled to pull their hair out.

MATT: Oh right. I didn't realise that was a thing.

SOPHIA: Well it is and it just got worse and worse.

TASH: So you didn't talk to the counsellor?

SOPHIA: I just felt like I was a problem that everyone was trying to fix. A big, fat inconvenience and my parents just wanted to pay someone to sort it out like they always did. So I told the counsellor what she wanted to hear. I felt better. I was stressed before but everything was okay now. She signed me off. I was fixed.

TASH: But you weren't.

SOPHIA: Nope. I don't think my parents knew what to do.

TASH: My mum wanted to help but I don't think she knew how. We'd go round and round in circles. She'd shout, I'd shout, she'd cry, I'd cry and then I'd storm out.

SCENE 24

TASH'S MUM: Tash, can you come in here please? We need to talk.

TASH: I've got homework Mum.

TASH'S MUM: Well this is important. Sit down.

TASH: You're always saying you want me to do my homework and then you stop me when I try.

TASH'S MUM: You can do it later. Please sit down.

TASH sits down in a huff.

TASH'S MUM: Right okay. So how are you? How are…things?

TASH: What? Is that it? That the best you got? I'm fine. Can I go to my room now?

TASH'S MUM: No. We said after what happened before that we'd be honest with each other and we'd talk.

TASH: Not this again. I'm fine.

TASH'S MUM: But you're not are you Tash?

TASH: What's that supposed to mean.

TASH'S MUM: I know you've done it again. I found some things in your room.

TASH: You've been going through my stuff!

TASH'S MUM: Tash. I was worried.

TASH: You said we would trust each other and then you go through my things?

TASH'S MUM: I had to Tash. You don't talk to me.

TASH: Well I don't want to. I'm fine okay. Why can't we just leave it at that?

TASH'S MUM: Because I can't let you go on hurting yourself without doing anything about it.

TASH: Why not? It's my body. Why does it make the slightest difference to you what I do with it?

TASH'S MUM: You need to stop it Tash.

TASH: Well I don't want to okay. I like it. It makes me feel better. Just cause you're too stuck in your own head to understand that.

TASH'S MUM: I'm trying to understand.

TASH: But you can't. My whole life I've felt like I'm sort of numb, stuck in some kind of fog, and when I do that it makes me feel something and I like it okay.

TASH'S MUM: Tash. It's not okay. You can't keep doing it. It's not healthy.

TASH: Says who?

TASH'S MUM: Well it's just not.

TASH: It's not up to you. You always taught me it was my body and I could decide what to do with it.

TASH'S MUM: Yes, but I was talking about not letting people touch you if you didn't feel ready not…

TASH: But it is my body?

TASH'S MUM: Well obviously. I just wish you'd respect it more.

TASH: So now you're saying I haven't got any self respect?

TASH'S MUM: Well not like that. I just want you to…

TASH: Well that's just it. What you want not what I want. I'm fine as I am.

TASH'S MUM: Tash, you're not. This isn't normal.

TASH: Great. So now I feel like a complete freak.

TASH'S MUM: Tash you know I didn't mean…

TASH: Thanks a lot Mum. That's just brilliant.

TASH'S MUM: Look, I'm not going over this again. This has to stop. You have to stop doing it.

TASH *leaves.*

TASH'S MUM: Tash, don't walk away from me. Tash!

SCENE 25

SOPHIA: I'm not sure what's worse. Talking about it too much or not at all?

MATT: It's definitely worse keeping it all bottled up. Wasn't there anyone you could talk to?

TASH: I had Yas.

SOPHIA: I talked to my physics teacher Dr. Silverberg. He was really helpful.

MATT: Your physics teacher?

SOPHIA: Yeah. I couldn't stand my house mistress so…

TASH: Are you really good at physics?

SOPHIA: Nope I'm rubbish. I just felt like I could talk to him.

MATT: Of all the people in the world you chose your male physics teacher!

SOPHIA: I know he wasn't the obvious choice. It doesn't really matter who you tell as long as you tell someone you trust.

SCENE 26

DR. SILVERBERG: Sophia, are you okay?

MATT: That's Doctor Silverberg?

SOPHIA: Yeah and..?

MATT: He's just not how I imagined him.

TASH: Shh.

SOPHIA: *(To* **DR. S.***)* I'm okay.

DR. SILVERBERG: Okay, but you know if you ever weren't okay you could talk to me.

SOPHIA: Yes, thank you.

  DR. SILVERBERG *goes to leave.* **SOPHIA** *suddenly blurts out.*

SOPHIA: I pulled my hair.

DR. SILVERBERG: Okay and is this the first time you've done this?

SOPHIA: No.

DR. SILVERBERG: And what made you do it this time?

SOPHIA: I saw a note the girls in my dorm were passing around.

TASH: I like how he hasn't just told her to stop it. He's actually trying to understand.

DR. SILVERBERG: And that hurt your feelings?

SOPHIA: Yes.

DR. SILVERBERG: How did it make you feel?

SOPHIA: Like I'm ugly.

DR. SILVERBERG: Okay. And when you've felt like this before how did you try to cope?

SOPHIA: I'd listen to my music.

DR. SILVERBERG: But it didn't work this time?

TASH: He's trying to help her to find positive coping mechanisms.

MATT: Yeah I know.

SOPHIA: I put my music on my headphones really loud and had a cry but Pandora saw me and told everyone so then I felt worse.

DR. SILVERBERG: So that's when you did it?

SOPHIA: Yes.

DR. SILVERBERG: Okay. And how did that make you feel?

SOPHIA: I felt better because for once I was in control.

DR. SILVERBERG: And did that feeling last?

SOPHIA: No! I felt ugly because I had this massive bald spot and my skin was really sore and I couldn't wear my hair how I like it.

DR. SILVERBERG: And then how did you feel?

SOPHIA: Like I'm fat, I'm ugly, like nobody wants to be seen with me.

DR. SILVERBERG: So you're back where you started?

SCENE 27

MATT: He was so calm and non judgmental.

SOPHIA: Yep he really helped me get better. I can be a bit over emotional.

TASH: We got that.

SOPHIA: Oi! He just made me see things differently.

TASH: It's like you have to teach your brain to think different thoughts.

SOPHIA: Yeah to think kinder thoughts.

TASH: I realised that I would never have treated someone else the way I was treating myself.

SOPHIA: Exactly.

MATT: So what made you get better?

TASH: My mum and my GP had tried to make me take these pills.

MATT: Anti-depressants?

TASH: Yeah. I didn't like the idea.

MATT: You weren't ready.

TASH: No. I used to say I'd taken them but not really take them. But eventually things got so bad that I had to talk to a doctor who made me realise that because I was depressed the chemicals in my brain were actually completely unbalanced and that was making it really hard for me to deal with my problem. It was like there was this quietness that just kind of wrapped itself around me.

MATT: The dementor's kiss.

SOPHIA: Will you quit going on about Harry Potter!

MATT: Sorry.

TASH: So once things were more balanced I was able to talk to a therapist. I had this thing called CBT.

MATT: Cognitive behavioural therapy. I had that.

TASH: Seriously?

SOPHIA: What's that?

TASH: It makes you aware of patterns in your behaviour and helps you to train your brain to think in more helpful ways.

SOPHIA: That's what Dr. Silverberg did for me. I realised that I was stuck in this horrible cycle and I couldn't break out of it.

MATT: Yep, know that feeling.

TASH: And me. The arguments with my mum used to drive me mad. It would all get too much and I'd run off crying.

SOPHIA: Where did you go?

SCENE 28

TASH arrives at YAS' front door.

TASH: Yas! Yas! It's me. Yas!

    YAS opens the door a little bit.

TASH: Well can I come in?

YAS: Sure. Shoes.

    TASH removes her shoes.

TASH: Yeah. Sorry. Your mum and dad not home?

    YAS checks the street and re-locks the door.

YAS: No not at the moment.

TASH: What time will they be coming home?

YAS: I'm not sure,

TASH: Can I sleep over?

YAS: What happened this time?

TASH: Arrhh. She just won't get off my case.

YAS: Well she's probably just worried.

TASH: No. She's interfering. All she ever says is stop doing it, stop doing it.

YAS: She might have a point. Have you done it again recently?

TASH: You sound like her. Don't you think if I could stop I would?

YAS: Show me.

    TASH reveals unpleasant septic looking burns.

YAS: Tash. That looks really nasty.

TASH: I know.

YAS: Let me look. Did you run it under the cold tap?

TASH: Yes.

YAS: For at least ten minutes?

TASH: Maybe not.

YAS: I think it's infected.

TASH: It's just a blister.

YAS: Tash don't. You'll make it worse. Take your watch off.

TASH: What?

YAS: In case it swells up. Right. We're going to the walk in centre first thing tomorrow. You might need antibiotics.

TASH: Oh Yas. Just leave it. I'm okay.

YAS: Okay fine we'll leave it. Don't blame me if you end up needing your arm amputated.

TASH: Amputated? Don't over react.

YAS: I'm not. If you leave a burn and let it get infected it can happen.

TASH: Oh you're a doctor now.

YAS: No.

TASH: Well how do you know?

YAS: I just know alright?

TASH: But something is weird in the way she's looking at me and I don't know why I push it with her but I do and suddenly it's all tumbling out. She's telling me about the city she lived in before she moved down here and her old school. She's telling me how she always loved learning and loved her school and had lots of friends. Then, the summer before she moved up to secondary she decided she wanted to wear the headscarf.

YAS: My mum wore one and so it made sense to me to do the same. My Dad wasn't so sure but I told him,"Daddy, lots of my friends are going to the same school. They know we are Muslim. Why will they care if

57

I wear a scarf? It does not change who I am." So when September came I wore my scarf and walked into school with my head held high. But secondary school was not like being in the juniors. So many people, so many people with so much to say.

TASH: She's telling me that's when the bullying started and it just kept getting worse. The comments and nasty looks quickly turned into physical threats and violence. Kids calling her a traitor or a terrorist.

YAS: And those friends from primary, they just looked the other way. They didn't want to get involved. My parents went to the school and some kids were excluded and every assurance was made that she would be safe. But teachers can't be looking all the time and friends of those excluded kids, they wanted revenge…

TASH: So they waited until no one was looking and there was no one to hear her cry and they surrounded her.

They held her still and demanded that she took off her scarf. When she refused one of the girls got out a lighter and said that they were going to burn her like a witch.

YAS: I don't know whether she intended what happened or just wanted to frighten me but as the naked flame was being waved by my face, I struggled and the flame caught my hijab and started to burn.

TASH: And she's telling me what burning flesh smells like. But then I already know.

She's telling me how they ran and left her whilst she screamed and cried and about the ambulance ride which she hardly remembers and the serious burns to her neck and arms and how she had to stay in hospital.

And I don't know what to say. And, whilst I should be thinking about her, how she's feeling, how she can possibly cope with something like that happening. I am not thinking about that. I'm thinking I'm a terrible friend for not knowing this sooner. I'm thinking I'm a fraud for burning myself when my closest friend has survived being burned alive. I'm thinking she'd be better off if it wasn't for me.

YAS: *(Beat.)* So I know my stuff with first aid okay? Promise me. We can go tomorrow.

TASH: Yas, I don't know what to say…

YAS: Tomorrow.

TASH: Okay. And I'm trying to think of something to say but there is nothing I can say so I don't say anything else and we don't speak about it again.

SCENE 29

SOPHIA: That's horrendous.

TASH: Yeah I know. The whole time she was listening to me whingeing when she'd been through something like that.

MATT: What a good friend.

TASH: Yeah the best.

SOPHIA: *(To MATT.)* Did you have anyone to talk to?

MATT: No one at school.

TASH: Not even what's her name? Hayley?

MATT: Especially not Hayley.

SCENE 30

MATT: So it's coming to the end of year 10 and stuff's starting to change. Things are starting to get serious. There's more homework and it's getting harder. Teachers keep telling us it's time to start knuckling down, that next year it'll be too late, and It's like I'm the only one who's noticed. Dan's still spinning his usual crap. Barry's still buying it. Chloe's still spending half her time in the loos reapplying her slap and Hayley, well Hayley, she seems to be doing really, really well.

And Miss Knight's giving us back our maths mocks and everyone's looking at their grades.

DAN: Bugger.

BARRY: Ah crap.

DAN: What d'you get?

BARRY: 2

DAN: I raise you an almighty 1.

BARRY: Respect.

HAYLEY: Chlo. Chloe. What d'ou get?

CHLOE: 4.

HAYLEY: Me too.

CHLOE: Snap.

HAYLEY: What about you Bob?

*(Awkward **BOB** is absent mindedly makes an elaborate origami item from his exam paper).*

BOB: What?

CHLOE: What d'ou get in the exam?

BOB: Oh right. Err 9

CHLOE: What?

HAYLEY: *You* got a 9?

DAN: No way. Let me see that!

CHLOE: What about you Matt?

DAN: Yeah Matt, how'd it go?

HAYLEY: Matt?

BARRY: You alright Matt?

BOB: Mate?

MATT: And it's like everything spins into slow, slow motion. I'm getting out of my seat and I'm crossing to the door and Miss Knight's saying something and Dan's making some lame joke or another about diarrhoea and I'm running full pelt down the corridor and into the loos and I head for the cubicle and I lock the door.

And I think I might be dying. There's a pain in my chest and I can't get my breath and my heart's beating right out of my rib cage and my head is buzzing, and my heart is thumping and I feel sick in my stomach and then…

BOB: *(Knocking on the door.)* Matt. Matt? You okay?

MATT: It's Bob. And I try and sound normal. "Yeah, I just needed the loo. Go back to class mate." And he stands there for a bit then I see his feet move and hear his steps fade back up the corridor.

And I need to get it together. I need to calm down, get out of this toilet and go back to my class, make some excuse and get on with it. The longer I leave it the worse it will get but I'm thinking about that exam paper and my empty desk and the panic is starting to rise in me again and I need to get out of here, I need to get some air, I need to breathe.

So I unlock the toilet door. Walk past the urinals and into the corridor. I want to turn left and head back to class. I mean to. I really do. But instead I'm heading right and towards the front doors and I'm out the door and up to the gates.

And it's only when I'm halfway home that my head starts to clear and I realise what I've done. Crap. I've walked out of class and completely off campus. I'm officially truanting and I didn't even mean to. I know I should turn around, head back in and explain to Miss Knight. I know I should but I can't seem to program my body to do it. So I'm at the end of my road and at my own gate and I'm putting my key in the door and heading up the stairs to my bedroom when…

MATT'S MUM: Oh Matt? You're home. How was the exam?

MATT: What?

MATT'S MUM: The Maths mock. I thought you said you were getting the results today?

MATT: Oh yeah. It went fine. *(Pause.)* I got an 7.

MATT'S MUM: A 7. Matt that's wonderful. Just think if you're getting 7's now, just think how well you'll do when it comes to the real thing. That's brilliant Matt. I'm so, so proud of you.

MATT: And I escape to the bedroom and I lock the door.

SCENE 31

MATT: And that was the first time I did it. I cut myself.

TASH: Over a maths test?

MATT: I know it sounds really stupid.

TASH: It is really stupid.

MATT: It wasn't just the maths test. It was…I don't know okay. It was everything.

TASH: What did you get?

MATT: What?

TASH: In the maths test. What did you get?

MATT: I got a 4 okay.

SOPHIA: Well that's not so bad. At least you passed…

MATT: But I don't get 4s. I'm good at maths.

TASH: So you'd had an off day.

MATT: Whatever it was I'd just got in such a state and I couldn't find a way to let out how I was feeling. I needed to release it.

SOPHIA: Couldn't you tell your mum?

MATT: I'd just lied to her so I felt terrible.

TASH: Couldn't you tell a friend from school or something?

MATT: Nope.

TASH: People must have found out.

MATT: I did it in places people wouldn't see and bunked PE at school so no one saw me get changed.

SOPHIA: Yeah but didn't you and Hayley…you know?

MATT: We were only fifteen so we weren't exactly that physical. I mean everyone assumed we'd been doing it for ages but…

TASH: You weren't.

MATT: No. I mean we kissed and stuff but nothing more…

TASH: And you were okay with that?

MATT: Suited me just fine. I mean not that I wouldn't have liked to but I couldn't risk anyone finding out.

SOPHIA: Were you afraid they'd make you get help?

MATT: No. I was afraid of how they'd react.

TASH: In what way.

MATT: Oh come on. As soon as everyone finds out you've been self-harming that's it.

SOPHIA: No one wants to know?

MATT: Nope, everyone wants to know about it.

SCENE 32

MATT, HAYLEY *and the lads are eating lunch.*

HAYLEY: Well first she put this on Instagram.

They all look.

DAN: That's a bit full on.

HAYLEY: Yeah. So I wrote this.

They all look.

BARRY: Ouch!

HAYLEY: Yeah then this morning she comes in brazen as anything with a short sleeved shirt on. I mean you could see everything!

MATT: She's coming.

HAYLEY: Dan move your bag.

DAN: What?

HAYLEY: Put your bag on the seat.

DAN: Okay.

HAYLEY: Shh. Pretend we haven't seen her…

CHLOE: Hi. Erm. Hayley. Can we talk?

HAYLEY: *(Smirking.)* Well we already are.

CHLOE: Yeah, erm. I just wondered if maybe we could talk on our own?

HAYLEY: Whatever you've got to say you can say in front of my friends.

CHLOE: I just thought maybe you and I could…

HAYLEY: I haven't got anything to hide. Have you?

CHLOE: No…okay…err… I was just thinking…

HAYLEY: Well spit it out. We haven't got all day.

CHLOE: I was thinking it would be nice if perhaps we could hang around together some time like we used to.

HAYLEY: You want to hang around with us?

CHLOE: Yeah.

HAYLEY: Well when?

CHLOE: Lunch time. After school?

HAYLEY: We're busy.

CHLOE: I didn't say which day.

HAYLEY: I said we're busy.

CHLOE: But…

MATT: Look Chlo. It's getting a bit embarrassing really. Hayley's already said we're busy.

DAN: Yeah, have some self-respect.

MATT: Look you've obviously found plenty of other friends like you online so why don't you go and whinge to them instead eh? Hayley's tried to be a good friend but everyone's got their breaking point and this is hers. Take the hint. You're not wanted.

CHLOE *pauses then cries and runs off.*

SCENE 33

MATT: I didn't want to show you that.

TASH: I'm not surprised. You're a total hypocrite. You're busy making her life hell when she's already at rock bottom and you're going home and doing the self same thing.

MATT: Yeah well I kept mine a secret.

TASH: Oh and that makes it better does it?

MATT: Look I'm not saying what I did was right but at least I wasn't moping around the corridors, wearing too much eye make up and posting attention seeking pictures of my latest burn scars on instagram.

TASH: Well she obviously was depressed.

MATT: Well clearly but everyone thought she was just some drama queen.

TASH: Okay, let's say she was seeking attention. Can you blame her? You were too busy with your own crappy love lives and personal crises to even register her existence.

MATT: I know. I know. I feel terrible. If I could change it I would okay? But I can't.

SOPHIA: What do you mean you can't.

TASH: You can talk to her.

SOPHIA: So you were a prat. It's not too late to make it right.

MATT: Yes it is!

SOPHIA: What do you mean?

TASH: Matt, what happened?

MATT: Forget it. Look, I can't do this now.

SOPHIA: No way Matt, what happened to Chloe?

MATT: Look, what do you care anyway? We've only just met.

SOPHIA: Don't walk away from us Matt.

TASH: *(Having a sudden realisation.)* Oh my God.

SOPHIA: What?

TASH: *(Shouting after **MATT**.)* You're not talking about Chloe Foreman are you? Matt!

MATT: *(Suddenly turning around.)* You knew her?

TASH: No. Wow. Chloe Foreman.

MATT: Please don't do this.

SOPHIA: Who's Chloe Foreman?

TASH: You'd know her face. Everyone knows her face.

MATT: Please Tash.

SOPHIA: What are you talking about?

TASH: Her mum came to our school.

SCENE 34

CHLOE's mum comes to **TASH**'s school.

CHLOE'S MUM: My name is Sarah Foreman. Some of you might have seen me on the news. Most of you probably know that my daughter Chloe took her life three months ago. If you've read about her you may know that she had, for a long time, struggled with self-harm and an eating disorder, that she had become addicted to destructive websites and that she was bullied at school. I'd like to start by telling you some things that you might not know about my daughter.

Chloe was a talented designer who wanted to study fashion at university. Just last year she'd won a competition and the outfit she'd designed was worn by a top model in London Fashion week.

She played the guitar badly.

Chloe was a very loyal friend, a loving sister and daughter and always volunteered to look after her little brother. She always knew how to make me laugh. *(She falters.)* She was my best friend.

We first became aware of Chloe's self-harm when she was in year 10. One afternoon, while she was at school, I came home early and checked her laptop. I felt bad because I've always trusted her. In the end I wished I'd checked sooner.

That's when I realised that our beautiful, talented daughter was posting photo after photo of her poor shrunken and damaged young body and receiving hundreds of comments from sick strangers who were logging on encouraging her to hurt herself.

I confiscated her laptop and her mobile. We took her to the doctor and we all went together for therapy as a family. I just couldn't understand why she'd want to do it. I begged her to stop.

She had eight weeks off of school.

I would watch her all the time to make sure she was safe. I checked on her in the middle of the night. I searched her drawers and her handbag.

We even disconnected the Wi-Fi.

As the weeks went by Chloe seemed more like herself.

She hadn't done it for a while and she'd started to put on weight.

Our therapist suggested that we give Chloe more freedom and let her have some online privileges and privacy. She kept telling me she needed to live in the real world so I gave in.

Less than two months later I went in to give Chloe a good night kiss and found that she had killed herself. That's it. Seven weeks was all the time it took for them to get at her again.

And I'm telling you this because absolutely nothing good can come from what happened to Chloe. No words can bring her back but I thought, maybe, if I can just make your generation more aware or stop one teenager from following Chloe's path, then it will have been worth speaking up.

Any questions?

TASH: And we all just sit there. No one knows what to say. There is this horrible awkward silence. We all know about self-harm and internet safety or we think we do but hearing it like this, from someone's mum, it's just different. This sort of thing doesn't happen at school. Adults don't walk into our school and tell the truth like that, so blatantly. Adults don't walk into our school and openly cry in front of the whole year. No one knows what to say and then Yas is putting her hand up.

CHLOE'S MUM: Yes.

TASH: And Yasmin's standing up and my heart is beating in my mouth.

YAS: Firstly I am so sorry for your loss and I thank you sincerely on behalf of all of us for sharing your experience with us.

TASH: And no one even sniggers.

YAS: I just wanted to ask you, if that's ok, how did you react when you first found out Chloe was self-harming?

CHLOE'S MUM: I was angry. I just couldn't understand why someone who had everything going for her would want to do that. I was furious with her.

YAS: Because you thought she was pathetic for doing such a thing?

TASH: And everyone thinks that Yas has overstepped the mark now. The teacher makes a move as though to silence her and some people start muttering but Chloe's mum puts out her hand to stop them and…

CHLOE'S MUM: No. It's a fair question. That's what Chloe thought. She thought I was angry because I thought she was being stupid, or pathetic or self-indulgent but I was angry because I felt helpless. I didn't think she was pathetic. I thought she was wonderful. I just wanted to help her so badly. I know that the problem wasn't actually the self-harm but the feelings underneath it but I wasn't scared of the feelings. It was the harming that freaked me out. I didn't know what to do so I lectured her and nagged her and kept telling her to stop. I was scared that she was going to go too far harming herself and my fear was justified.

TASH: And Yas thanks the woman and sits down. Her gaze hardly lingers on mine but she and I both know what she's done. With absolute subtlety, style and grace, she's made me see my mum in a whole different light and I want to run out there and then and run home and give my poor mum a hug but I don't 'cause I can't. I can't draw attention. But something is changing inside of me and I'm thinking I'm gonna beat this thing and I'm thinking my mum's going to help me. And for the first time in a really long time, I actually feel positive.

And Yas has broken the tension and the questions come thick and fast now and Chloe's mum's explaining about helplines and safe websites. And we're all listening cause how could you not listen when someone is telling you that the number of children and teenagers who have to go to A and E for self-harm is at an all-time high and that 1 in 5 fifteen year olds say they have self-harmed in the last year.

And the bell's ringing and Miss is thanking Chloe's mum and is dismissing us a row at a time and almost no one is speaking but I am changed.

SCENE 35

TASH: I am definitely going to go home and talk to my mum. I'm going to go home and apologise and say I will go to the doctor.

But first I need to thank Yas for what she's done so I'm looking for her at the bus stops and she's not there. And I'm thinking that's a bit weird cause normally she waits for me but Mum's not back from work for an hour so I can spare the time. So I'm making a detour to Yas' house before I go straight back home. I'm thinking maybe I'll buy my mum flowers or I'll cook her dinner so it's ready when she gets back.

But then I get to Yas' house and everything's wrong. There's flashing lights and sirens and the police have cordoned it all off and I can see smoke. And I hear myself screaming her name, screaming for Yas, but the police won't let me through and I'm turning and I'm walking away.

And I'm traveling home in a blur.

And I'm not picking up flowers.

And I'm not putting the dinner on.

And I am heading straight to the medicine cabinet.

SCENE 36

TASHA's *house.*

TASH'S MUM: Tash. You home? Tash? Oh my God. Tash, Tash. Talk to me. Christ Tash. Hello, hello. Ambulance. It's my daughter she's not conscious. Please come quickly. She's fifteen. Tash!

TASH: And I'm hearing everything she's saying but I can't talk back. And time is moving at a weird dreamlike pace.

TASH'S MUM: God yes. She's in here. Hurry please.

PARAMEDIC 1: What's her name?

TASH'S MUM: Tash. It's Tasha. Oh God!

PARAMEDIC 2: Tash. Tasha. Can you hear me?

TASH'S MUM: Oh my God. Oh my God.

PARAMEDIC 2: Open your eyes.

PARAMEDIC 1: How old is she?

TASH'S MUM: She's fifteen. Oh God. Oh God.

PARAMEDIC 1: Do you know if she's taken anything?

(*TASHA starts to make a retching noise.*)

PARAMEDIC 2: Okay Tash. We're just going to pop you on your side in case you're going to be sick.

TASH'S MUM: Erm. I don't know. Oh God.

PARAMEDIC 1: Is she on any regular medication?

TASH'S MUM: She has anti-depressants.

PARAMEDIC 1: Could you get them?

TASH'S MUM: Right. Yes. I think so. Is she okay? Is she going to be okay?

PARAMEDIC 2: Okay Tash we're going to move you onto a stretcher so you can go in the ambulance okay. We're going to move you on three okay? 1, 2, 3.

PARAMEDIC 1: Are these her pills?

TASH'S MUM: Yes. Oh Tasha. Wake up! Please wake up!

PARAMEDIC 1: Okay, we're going to take you both to the hospital. Do you have your house keys?

TASH'S MUM: What?

PARAMEDIC 1: You need your house keys, phone, anything else you might need.

TASH'S MUM: Right.

PARAMEDIC 1: I think maybe you should put some shoes on.

TASH'S MUM: Right yes.

PARAMEDIC 2: Okay Tash. Just a quick ride to St George's okay?

TASH: And as I hear the sirens start to wail, my mum completely loses it.

*(**TASH**'s mum sobs.)*

SCENE 37

TASH: Yas, are you…?

YAS: Shh. Your mum's just talking to the doctor.

TASH: But what happened?

YAS: Don't try to speak…

TASH: Your house…

YAS: Shhhh.

TASH: And she's telling me how when she left the assembly hall her mum was waiting at the gate for her. She's telling me how there *was* a fire but at a house at the end of her road and her mum had come to get her because she thought she might freak out.

She's telling me how they went to get some dinner and how while they were out she called me and my mum picked up my mobile and told her I was here. She insisted her mum brought her straight over.

(To **YAS**.*)* So the fire…?

YAS: An electrical fault.

TASH: It was nothing to do with…

YAS: No.

TASH: But I thought. I thought it had happened again.

YAS: Not everything stays the same. Some things change.

TASH: *(She breaks down.)* I'm so sorry.

YAS: What for?

TASH: For being selfish. For banging on about my problems when you had problems of your own.

YAS: It's not a competition Tash and you are not selfish. You felt horrible enough about yourself to need to do this. It wouldn't matter to me if you were upset because you'd broken your fingernail or broken your neck. The fact is you were upset. That's all that mattered.

TASH: But…

YAS: Seriously I mean it.

TASH: I'm sorry I wasn't a better friend.

YAS: You were. You were the best friend I could possibly have had. You can't be there for someone if they won't let you.

TASH: What happens now?

YAS: It's time for your life to change.

TASH: I don't know if I…

YAS: You can.

TASH: And I'm looking at Yas, brave, beautiful, wise beyond her years Yas and my mum's coming in her face red raw from crying and I know that Yas is right. It's time for me to get the help I need. It will be hard but, with them by my side, I know I can do it.

SCENE 38 – FESTIVAL – EPILOGUE

MATT: So slowly

SOPHIA: A little bit at a time.

TASH: Things actually got better.

MATT: And I started to count the days since I last did it.

TASH: And the numbers got bigger.

SOPHIA: Days, into weeks and into months.

TASH: And sometimes I still have to check myself.

MATT: Old habits are hard to break.

SOPHIA: I have to stop myself from going there again but I know that if I ever do. Don't worry I won't.

TASH: You better not.

SOPHIA: I know that if I do I'll be able to get myself out again.

MATT: It was no good thinking I'll just stop because I didn't know how to.

TASH: But with help from my friend and my psychiatrist.

SOPHIA: From my teacher.

MATT: From my mum.

TASH: We broke the cycle and ended up here…

MATT: In a field.

SOPHIA: At a fantastic festival.

TASH: In the long summer after GCSEs.

MATT: If we can do it. You can too.

MATT: And I'm actually really happy because I'm not *that* person…

TASH: *That* girl

MATT: *That* boy

SOPHIA: *That* attention seeking girl I'm just

TASH: Tash

SOPHIA: Sophia

MATT: Matt

TASH: So that's it. Our play

SOPHIA: It was about self-worth

MATT: Mental health

SOPHIA: And self-harm.

MATT: 'Cause we're not hiding any more.

They dance.

Salamander Street

Teachers – if you are interested in buying a set of texts for your class please email info@salamanderstreet.com – we would be happy to discuss discounts and keep you up to date with our latest publications and study guides.

<u>Also available from Nina Lemon</u>

Losing It
A Play about Coming Together and Falling Apart
Paperback 9781913630560
eBook 9781913630553

Teachers' Packs for *Hidden* and *Losing It* are available for download from Salamander Street.

Follow us on Twitter or Facebook or visit our website for the latest news.